SEEDS OF RECOVERY

A Journal of 101 Mental Health Reflections

LORETTE M. ENOCHS

authorHOUSE®

AuthorHouse™
1663 Liberty Drive
Bloomington, IN 47403
www.authorhouse.com
Phone: 1 (800) 839-8640

Published by AuthorHouse 11/19/2016

ISBN: 978-1-5246-5182-4 (sc)
ISBN: 978-1-5246-5181-7 (e)

Print information available on the last page.

Any people depicted in stock imagery provided by Thinkstock are models,
and such images are being used for illustrative purposes only.
Certain stock imagery © Thinkstock.

This book is printed on acid-free paper.

Because of the dynamic nature of the Internet, any web addresses or links contained in
this book may have changed since publication and may no longer be valid. The views
expressed in this work are solely those of the author and do not necessarily reflect the
views of the publisher, and the publisher hereby disclaims any responsibility for them.

This book is dedicated to Dr. Entezari, my therapist who supported me through my most difficult times and my children who inspired me to be well: Shannon, Andrew, and Quinn.

Belonging To:

Acknowledgements

Special thanks to Drs. Kathleen Heide and Kathleen McNeill PhD.,
Leslie Kern, R.N., Karen McKenna, Ellen Reedy, and Eleanor Arntzen,
I am indebted to Dara Elerath for her graphic art.

Preface

One out of seventeen people has a serious mental illness interrupting his/her life. Mental illness is an equal opportunist affecting individuals regardless of ethnicity, gender, intellectual capability, or income. Recovery from mental illness is real. Recovery is not a cure. It means living a rewarding and contributing life by finding coping skills that aid us through our most difficult times. There is no one path for recovery. Recovery happens through a smorgasbord of choices, beginning with acceptance. Through acceptance we acknowledge that our emotions or thoughts have been extreme and those extreme thoughts or emotions interfered with our relationships—relationships with family members, self, partners, friends, and co-employees. Mental illness may have created financial and legal problems for us. In recovery, we choose to seek information and assistance that will lead us to a more rewarding life.

We can find relief from a variety of recovery choices: psychiatrists, psychologists, peer support, and supplemental treatments. Group or individual counseling may benefit some. Art and music therapy may touch the souls of some people in recovery and lead to the necessary changes to create fulfilling lives. Some turn to journaling for expressing their emotions and thoughts. *Seeds of Recovery: A Journal of 101 Mental Health Reflections* is a compilation of inspirational quotes and my thoughts about recovery. It offers the reader the opportunity to write their insights about his or her individual recovery journey. By reflecting upon quotes, interpretations, and affirmations, the reader can then begin writing their own beliefs

and observations concerning his/her recovery experience. A journal of this kind is an experiential tool in the recovery process. The expression of one's recovery is not limited to writing. The page next to the reflection can used for drawing or gluing photos or making collages. The empty spaces of the lotus lend to using color ink pens to produce a barometer of your feelings. Therapists may find it helpful to begin a group discussion based upon quotes and the interpretation of the quotes. Groups may begin or end a session with the wise words found in this book. For those of you who are receiving this book electronically, you may want to express yourself in a notebook.

Seeds of Recovery was written for individuals living with mental illness regardless of diagnosis, and its topics resonate with individuals who seek recovery. The book addresses hope, resiliency, courage, grieving, losses, setbacks, self-love, and self-help. The text and affirmations after each quote are written from my heart and based upon my experiences.

Other individuals who are living with mental illness have graciously read what I have written and encouraged me to share my insights with others.

Until the lion has his or her own storyteller, the hunter will always have the best part of the story.—African proverb

People who seek recovery are heroes for combating the invisible demons that torture their thoughts and feelings. Their journeys to find serenity are plagued with obstacles. These heroes have unique stories of courage and determination to tell. It is important that we become our own storyteller; otherwise, the individuals who are ignorant and prejudice about mental illness will prevail in society. Our stories of recovery offer hope to others living with mental illnesses and family members. We, in recovery, are the harbingers of change and living witnesses to the recovery movement.

Sharing our heroic stories in a safe environment can be very powerful for both the listener and speaker.

The soul that is within me no man can degrade.—Frederick Douglass

We are persons living with mental illnesses. If you think less of us because of the biochemical fragility of our brains, let it be known that your degrading words shall not touch our souls. Come live in our heads; experience the frightening and confusing delusions; ride our roller-coaster moods; be jolted to our past traumas; listen to the constant chattering of voices that invade our minds. Our recovery and resiliency to deal with these difficulties are testimonies to our strength. Lack of compassion is born of fear—fear that you would not have the courage and strength to endure our struggles. Through understanding, we forgive.

I will not allow others to degrade my soul. I recover because I was given the gift of resiliency.

When it is dark enough, you can see the stars.—Anonymous

We who live with mental illnesses know that our moods and behaviors turn extreme during the darkest depths of our disorders, inhibiting our ability to function well. But it is during such dark periods that the stars of hope for recovery will shine. We who are on the path of recovery offer encouragement to those who have been recently diagnosed. We know that a good life after diagnosis is possible. We have given meaning to our lives and to other people's lives.

The stars of hope will guide me during my darkest hours.

The soul would have no rainbow if the eyes had no tears.—John Vance Cheney

Many of us living with mental illnesses have taken frightening and confusing emotional journeys beyond all known galaxies involving intermittent intrusions of mood swings, delusions, flashbacks, anxiety, mania, or hallucinations, and returned to the here and now to tell of our odysseys. We can choose to curse these enigmatic excursions of the mind and moods or rejoice in our recovery or do both. Anger and grieving are normal reactions after learning that we have a diagnosis. Recovery allows us to rejoice.

Recovery is an extraordinary power in my life. It is a rainbow of the soul.

Water is fluid, soft, and yielding. But water will wear away rock, which is rigid and cannot yield. As a rule, whatever is fluid, soft, and yielding will overcome whatever is rigid and hard.—Lao-Tzu

Mental illness is not anyone's fault. Randomly, biochemical differences or trauma occurred that caused us to think, feel, or act differently and more extremely at times. Our life journeys run like the mighty Rio Grande twisting through lush, green valleys, and desert canyons and flowing peacefully into pools. But when we experience the turbulence of mental illness, it is like the rapids of the river, colliding with boulders and sometimes overflowing the banks, requiring cleanup and rebuilding. Our lives changed course twice: the day that our symptoms erupted and the day we set foot on the path of recovery. We learn to respond to crisis and improve our lives by discovering the fluid path of recovery.

I will follow the fluid, soft and yielding path of recovery.

When practicing unconditional acceptance, start with yourself.—Lo-jong proverb

Although we cannot alter the reality of our diagnosis, we can alter our attitude concerning our diagnosis to one of acceptance. Acceptance rarely roars. It usually whispers so listen closely. Acceptance of our diagnosis offers the possibility of recovery for those of us living with mental illnesses. With acceptance, we can step onto the path to recovery that ensures us a better life, offering greater possibilities for lasting relationships and fulfilling our dreams.

I will listen closely to my heart guiding me into acceptance and recovery.

Beauty is not in the face; beauty is a light in the heart.—
Kahlil Gibran

Time away from television, family, or friends gives us opportunities for finding inner enlightenment. The stillness of a lake, the silence of an empty park, or the gentleness of a soft wave rolling up to the beach opens us to finding our inner beauty. If you cannot go to such places imagine yourself there. Take deep breaths, relaxing as you inhale and exhale. Visualize a serene lake, tree-filled park, or a beach with gentle waves. Then tell yourself that the light in your heart is more beautiful than any imagined place. That is the truth.

The light in my heart is more beautiful than any place that I could imagine.

Everyone has been made for some particular work, and the desire for that work has been put in every heart.— Jalal ad-Din Muhammad Rumi

Most people yearn to work. Work often gives people a sense of worth. People living with a mental illness have a right to work and reasonable accommodation is the law. When will the world embrace those of us living with mental illnesses? Perhaps the day may come when we see advertisements such as, "Hiring Those Who Live with Mental Illnesses." Since one in four persons had a mental health need some time in their lives, competition would be stiff. We remain silent about our conditions for fear that stigma due to prejudices and misunderstandings about mental illness exists in the workplace and would interfere with our employment. Prejudices and misunderstandings are not our fault. Mental illnesses are not our fault. We will live with the hope that one day we will find meaningful work despite such prejudices and misunderstandings.

I will assess my capabilities, set my goals accordingly, and not allow naysayers to squelch my desire to work.

Humor invites sanity and heals the wounds of mental illnesses. LME

Time and distance from the depths of where our illnesses have taken us, allow us to view our lives in a kaleidoscope of color, transforming darkness into the beauty of recovery. Humor can both assist and be a measure of our healing.

My sense of humor heals me.

The mystery of life is not a problem to be solved but a reality to be experienced.—Aart Van der Leeuw

We often believe that mental illness is something that only happens to other people until it happens to us. Then we wonder why depression, post-traumatic stress syndrome, schizophrenia, obsessive-compulsive disorder, bipolar disorder, borderline personality disorder happened to us when life held so many promises for us—friends, education, professions, and dreams. One day scientists may be able to explain how the biochemical "juices" of the brain or traumatic life experiences cause the mood swings, hallucinations, OCD, anxiety, flashbacks, or delusions, but the puzzle still remains: Why us? We will never know the answer to this question. Look beyond this mystery, and find consolation in knowing that we are strong enough to cope with a condition that has the ability to distort our thoughts or moods and to combat societal prejudices associated with the words mental illness. We can choose to accept that the greater mystery of life is a reality to be experienced and that our lives have meaning despite having been diagnosed with a mental illness.

I relish my life and accept its difficulties—I have meaning.

Man is the only critter who feels the need to label things as flowers or weeds.—Anonymous

For medical purposes, clinicians attach inadequate words such as bipolar disorder, schizophrenia, post-traumatic stress disorder, schizoaffective disorder, or clinical depression to the extraordinary mental and emotional journeys we travel as a result of the biochemical imbalances of the brain. But such terms do not sufficiently express our experiences, which are both unique and universal. We may not understand why our minds have traveled a different path, but we shall dance down our path carrying our own colorful umbrella of recovery.

I will always rebel at being labeled, but if others must label me, call me a person in recovery.

We can secure other people's approval, if we do right and try hard; but our own is worth a hundred of it, and no one way has been found out of securing that.—Mark Twain

Approval is a common need for all people. The pursuit of approval is lifelong and rooted in ego. On occasions we don't care about the source of approval or how we achieve it, but we relish its intoxicating effect. We believe that if only we try hard enough, our reward will be a pat on the back, an award, recognition, or applause. But eventually we learn that the greatest approval that we can receive is self-approval. Self-approval is an oasis of inner peace in a desert of insecurity.

I will be an oasis of self-approval.

Serenity comes when you trade expectations for acceptance.—Anonymous

Mental illness is a life-altering lesson for our families and us—never did we anticipate that our futures would revolve around whatever it takes to achieve and maintain wellness. After all, we expected a much different life. But the course of our lives has been altered. We pop antipsychotics and antidepressants, or benzodiazepines like other people pop vitamins in the morning. We find our friends at groups, where we share our common experiences. Our acceptance allows us to tolerate mood swings, flashbacks, hallucinations, mania, anxiety, disorganized thoughts, or delusions that intrude into our lives. We seek serenity by forgiving our extreme behavior and acknowledging that it was the result of our neurotransmitters gone awry or trauma descending into our lives.

Acceptance, wellness, and serenity are also life-altering lessons.

You were born with wings. Why prefer to crawl through life?—Jalal ad-Din Muhammad Rumi

We often curse the trickster of hereditary or environmental catalysts that ensured us a destiny with mental illness and seemingly clipped our wings by attempting to steal our dreams. Without dreams there is only resignation to a life as is. But we cannot accept our life as others might condemn it. If we must struggle more than others to achieve, then we will. Our glory and achievement is more splendorous because of our struggles. Although mental anguish may impede our journey, we will not let this invisible interloper succeed in discouraging us. Stigma, ignorance, and intolerance are roadblocks to success, but to borrow from the powerful motto of the civil rights movement: "We shall overcome."

I accept nothing but success—one step at a time whether it is a baby step, shuffle step, or moon walk.

You've got approval.—Susan Ness

We are keenly aware of ignorant and cruel judgments from those who have never experienced madness. The whispers usually begin, "She/he is schizophrenic or bipolar." Such stigmatizing language can cause isolation, fear, and shame. If only people would be so kind as to distinguish between the disorder and the person. Maybe we cannot silence the stigmatizing whispers but we can fight ignorance and cruelty by living good lives despite bad circumstances. Being aware of cruel judgments from some, we who are in recovery have learned to rely upon ourselves for approval. We can find hope and success in our progress. We can forgive ourselves for missteps and remember that tomorrow brings a new day.

I've got self-approval!

It's never too late to become what you might have been.— George Eliot

Society measures us by our worth to society such as being a doctor, lawyer, clothes designer, soldier, police officer, scientist, ball player, engineer, nurse, singer, or actor. Undeniably, some careers are unattainable because of our disability (ability to be different). Security clearances and certifications are often denied even before the ink is dry on our applications for admission to exclusive employment leagues. Yet, some of us living with mental illnesses are nurses, lawyers, doctors, psychologists, and engineers. Others whose disabilities have impacted them more severely contribute by volunteering in hospices, nursing homes, daycare centers, treatment centers, or groups. Such volunteer opportunities can be just as fascinating and rewarding as the career paths we might have otherwise followed. For it is in giving and sharing of our life experiences that we become what we really intended to be even if we take a different route. True worth is defined by our willingness to enrich other people's lives.

I will find a way to enrich other people's lives by giving and sharing my experiences.

No feeling is final.—Rainer Maria Rilke

While we are experiencing the extreme feelings that are root of our debilitation, it may seem as though our emotional thermostat will never budge. But we must remember that our emotions are normal; it is their depth and duration that differentiates us from others. With support and time, our moods and thoughts will change and we can learn to manage our extreme emotions and perceptions.

Life, by definition, is in constant motion. I realize that my emotions will change for the better and my life will improve.

Not to laugh, not to lament, not to judge, but to understand.—Baruch Spinoza

We who live with mental illnesses choose to reject pity, contempt, or judgment. No one should judge us, not even others with mental illnesses, for each person's journey differs from that of others. But, we do ask for understanding and compassion. Compassion and understanding are knowledge-based qualities shared among equals. We, also, need to give ourselves some compassion with the hope that others may follow suit.

My need for understanding and compassion is universal and I shall graciously accept it from all sources.

He that conceals his grief finds no remedy for it.—Turkish proverb

We who live with mental illnesses have experienced losses such as finances, freedom, relationships, or work. To be well, we live vigilant lives of recovery, sometimes requiring limitations. Our limitations are frustrating. We heal our painful and frustrating experiences through grief. Inexplicably, grieving heals the wounds of losses and limitations. By grieving, we take the first steps toward recovery.

Rather than conceal my grief caused by losses and limitations, I will find a safe environment to express it, thereby jump-starting my recovery.

Be not afraid of growing slowly, be afraid only of standing still.—Chinese proverb

Recovery is hard work, requiring courage, faith and action; however, the rewards are great. Even though our recovery progress is slow at times, we will move our lives forward from being nearly crippled to establishing better relationships—financial, familial, interpersonal, and employment. Recovery allows us to celebrate the joy of our returned sanity.

My faith and my courage to recover propel me into action.

You yourself, as much as anybody in the entire universe, deserve your love and affection.—Buddha

The diagnoses of schizophrenia, bipolar disorder, schizoaffective disorder, borderline personality disorder, general anxiety, and other mental illnesses have shaken the core of our being. Our symptoms during our worst times seem to overpower us. But we can and do overcome the urge to feel defeated by our disorders. We begin by reminding ourselves that we are not our diagnosis—we are individuals with the same capacity to love and be loved as anyone else and we deserve love.

I will flood my being with loving-kindness, opening possibilities for loving relationships.

Our sorrows and wounds are healed only when we touch them with compassion.—Buddha

Confronting our diagnosis is an unending, daily battle. We work to keep our true being out of harm's way. Through self-awareness, self-forgiveness, and self-compassion, we can let go of the difficult past and heal our emotional wounds clearing the way for a future where we experience our daily triumphant over the isolation and confusion caused by mental illness. Self-compassion heals our emotional wounds—wounds that spring from the bio-chemical imbalances of our brain or from those who cruelly judge us. Our determination to heal our sorrows and wounds opens the path to life's possibilities.

I will heal my sorrows and wounds through self-compassion.

Purpose serves as a principle around which to organize our lives.—Anonymous

Although for those living with mental illness the path to inner peace is fraught with difficulties, having a strong purpose of recovery gives us a principle around which to organize our lives and dissipate the torments of our mind. Even though it is hard to accept that everything, including mental illness has a purpose, we who live with a mental illness do have a purpose to our lives. Our presence reminds others of the fragility of the brain; our recovery offers hope.

Recovery gives me a purpose while my life serves the purpose of showing others that recovery is possible.

A faithful friend is the medicine of life.—Apocrypha

When our symptoms are at their worst, a friend stands by us. He or she cares about our wellbeing, encouraging us to seek the resources necessary to restore wellness. A friend is one who cares for us despite the surfacing of our debilitating symptoms. A friend stands by us as we unwillingly venture into the darkness of our disorders and offers us patience, hope, and encouragement. Our friend's acceptance is the strongest ally on our path of recovery. I am my own best friend.

I am blessed for I am a friend unto myself.

With time and patience, the mulberry leaf becomes a silk gown.—Chinese proverb

Mental illness can be debilitating, negatively impacting our relationships, work, or finances. But mental illness does not stagnate. We can transform our condition into mental wellness with support and treatment. Recovery requires time, patience, effort, and determination. We who live in recovery are monuments of courage and determination.

I think and know that I can improve my life through patience and determination.

do not exist. —Queen Victoria

We are not interested in the possibilities of defeat. They do not exist.—Queen Victoria

The word defeat does not exist in the vocabulary of recovery. Although our road to recovery is neither straight nor flat but instead winding and bumpy, it is possible to traverse it successfully. With treatment, therapy, and vigilance, we are able to conquer or manage our anxiety, depression, flashbacks, mania, hallucinations, or delusions and participate in life-affirming activities such as work and healthy relationships. We must never give up hope in our recovery. Recovery exists for us all.

I will never accept defeat or give up the hope of recovery.

He who suffers much will know much.—Greek proverb

A biochemical imbalance or trauma has caused us to suffer. However, because of our suffering we have a greater appreciation of happiness. We don't take happiness for granted, knowing it can be as fleeting as a shooting star. So when it appears in our lives, we embrace it, recognizing how it enriches us.

My suffering has not been in vain; I have a greater appreciation for the moments of happiness in my life.

LORETTE M. ENOCHS

". . .what is happening in your innermost self is worthy of your entire love, somehow you must find a way to work at it .—Rainer Maria Rilke

Regardless of the confusion, debilitation, or extraordinary emotion caused by our trauma or biochemical imbalance, we are individuals who are worthy of our love. Love forgives and accepts our inabilities. We should listen to our soft, inner voice of self-love that reminds us that no one is perfect, forgiveness heals, and we deserve love.

I am worthy of my love and love from others.

Do what you can, with what you have, where you are.—
Theodore Roosevelt

There are no superwomen or supermen. They are ideals. Comparisons with the ideals only result in disappointments. We can only be expected to do what we can with what we have and where we are at a given moment. Success is defined differently for everyone just as the course of mental illness is different for everyone. For some people, success will be getting out of bed and eating. For others success may be a trip to the grocery store. For still others success may be working part time or full time.

We are heroes every day for doing what we can with what we have, and where we are.

When you do a thing, do it with all your might. Put your whole soul into it.—Ralph Waldo Emerson

No one can draw us a map to our recovery. We have to draw it ourselves through successes and failures and punctuate it with our own personalities and energy. By putting our whole soul into following our recovery map, we will discover wellness one day. It is okay if on certain days we only have a small amount of energy to spare for our recovery. Every step that we take toward recovery supports hope for a better tomorrow and wellness.

I will put my whole soul into achieving wellness one step at a time.

Make the best use of what is in your power, and take the rest as it happens.—Epicetus

As our diagnosis first rings in our ears, we are confused and unwilling to have a psychological label associated with our behavior. This can't happen to me! Our willingness to accept our mental illness, which is within our power, often defines how well we will live our lives. When we are able to accept our diagnosis, we are open to the steps of recovery: education, treatment, support, and therapy. Through education we learn of others who have achieved their dreams despite their diagnosis. Education, which is in our power, strengthens our hope and resolve for success and enlightens us about how to improve our lives.

I will make the best use of what is in my power through my willingness to accept my diagnosis and educate myself about recovery.

Your worth consists in what you are and not in what you have.—Thomas Edison

Our worth is reflected in our resiliency and strength, which are more important in our recovery than affluence. When assessing our wealth, reflect on how well we endure the distortions of our emotions and thinking and rise to the challenge of recovery. Some of us treasure our mental wellness while others who are new to recovery treasure the day that mental wellness will enter their lives.

I rejoice in the riches of resiliency and strength that support my recovery.

Lorette M. Enochs

Tell a person they are brave and you help them become so.—Thomas Carlyle

Combating the effects of our conditions—fighting stigma, isolation, and misunderstanding—requires courage. We battle our raging symptoms like a soldier confronts the enemy on the battlefield—avoiding land mines that could result in traumatic consequences. Whoever tells us that we are heroes? Every mental health clinic and hospital should post a sign that says: "Only heroes walk through these doors." But even when others don't acknowledge our bravery we can do so. Acknowledging our own bravery helps us sustain our recovery.

I acknowledge my bravery and acknowledge that I live a heroic life.

Do we not all agree to call rapid thought and noble impulse by the name of inspiration?—George Eliot

In our world, rapid thinking and impulsive behavior, which we may erroneously believe to be noble, can be symptoms of our mental illness rather than inspiration. Impulsiveness can be admired and rewarded or feared and ridiculed. Words such as impulsiveness and mental illness can conjure up value judgments. Mental illness is more often than not negatively perceived. Let's change the label of "mental illness" to inspiration and begin seeing ourselves as people living with inspiration. After all, we inspire courage, resiliency and recovery.

I will change any label that undermines my sense of self-worth and determination for recovery.

He who has hope has everything.—Arab proverb

In my mind, hope is an acronym for **H**armonious **O**ptimistic **P**owerful **E**nergy. Hope propels us in search for light despite our darkest moments. Sometimes we don't know how the spark of hope is kindled within us, but we're comforted by its presence as though wrapped in blankets on a freezing night. Hope transforms difficult moments, hours, days or weeks and moves us forward to a promising future. Listen to the **H**armonious **O**ptimistic **P**owerful **E**nergy stirring within, reminding us that we are on the path to recovery and our life in the future will be enhanced.

Hope is the most powerful tool in my recovery toolbox.

The most powerful weapon on earth is the human soul on fire—Ferdinand Foch

When we were told of our diagnosis, some of us experienced shock and denial while others were relieved to know that there was a label for our extreme thinking and behavior. Whether we were shocked or relieved, we all experienced pain as we realized that our lives had been altered by chemical imbalance or traumatic event. Nevertheless, we can embrace the wisdom that our most powerful weapon is our soul on fire, which ignites our desire to take steps toward recovery and create meaningful, productive lives.

I have a soul on fire to find meaningful, productive activities that will nurture and enlighten me.

Stars are not seen by sunshine.—Spanish proverb

We know the darkness of mental illness, which includes isolation, pain, and confusion. But even in our darkest days we can see the stars of hope that offer glimmers of bright possibilities for our futures. Those stars of hope guide us through our darkest moments, reminding us that recovery is possible and that life improves once we give treatment and support a chance.

During the times of darkness, I shall look for the star of hope to guide me in recovery.

One often calm's one's grief by recounting it.—Pierre Corneille

We have a right to grieve our losses. Mental illness takes a toll in our lives interfering with financial, familial, interpersonal, educational, or work relationships. By taking the time to grieve, we heal our wounds. The more we grieve, the more we heal. The more we heal the fuller is our recovery. The fuller our recovery, the more we can achieve.

My grief is a magical source for healing.

When spider webs unite, they can tie up a lion.—
Ethiopian proverb

When our illness is out of control, it roams like a hungry lion, indifferent to where, when, how, or whom it strikes next, even turning on us at times. But we seek wellness through our support systems and coping skills—such as forgiving ourselves because we realize that our behavior is due to the mixed up messages of our brains. When we are on the road to recovery utilizing our coping skills and support system, we are like the spider webs uniting to tie up the lion of our out-of-control illness.

I will utilize my coping skills and support system so I can move forward in my recovery.

What will come from the briar but the berry.—Irish proverb

Some may define mental illness, as a tangled briar patch of the mind from which there is no escape. But from this briar patch comes the berry of recovery. Recovery is a process achieved through hope, education, vigilance, and dedication and it is well worth the effort. It can be attained with the help of treatment and a support network. With recovery, we reclaim the ability to re-engage in healthy relationships with family, friends, or employers.

I will find the berry of recovery that grows from the briar patch of mental illness.

Lorette M. Enochs

If you do not know the way, walk slowly.—Irish proverb

Recovery doesn't happen overnight. Recovery is a lifelong process. Recovery requires effort—reaching out for education and learning through trial and error helps us rise like a phoenix from the ashes of our darkest moments. Full throttle and warp speed are only for spaceships—certainly not for recovery. We should give ourselves permission to move at a tortoise's speed when necessary, remembering that the tortoise won the race with the hare nonetheless. Recovery doesn't mean that we are free of our disorder—it means that our lives improved because of our willingness to nurture ourselves and seek support.

Until I'm familiar with the path of recovery, I will walk slowly and trust those who can guide me on my way.

Suppressed grief suffocates; it rages within the breast and is forced to multiply its strength.—Ovid

When we choose to suppress our grief from losses due to mental illness, we become suffocated, as our grief increases in strength. Expressing our emotions of grief in a safe environment helps us to close our painful wounds. Validation of that pain also sutures the wounds, allowing us to heal. Grief is a magical, powerful tool in our recovery and one that we should not disregard.

I will build a support network that will allow me to grieve and validate the hardship of mental illness, which will contribute to my healing.

Lorette M. Enochs

The person who says it cannot be done should not interrupt the person who is doing it.—Chinese proverb

People, who are skeptical about our ability to recover from mental illness, should move out of our way as we walk the road of recovery. Recovery doesn't mean that every day is a good day. Recovery means acknowledging the dark days, recognizing that nothing is constant, and having hope that tomorrow offers a better day. With strategies for making it through our most difficult periods, we are able to believe in a rewarding future.

I will not let my walk on the road to recovery be interrupted by skeptics.

Nothing is so burdensome as a secret.—French proverb

Often people prejudge us once they've learned that we have a mental illness. As a result, we remain silent about our disorders for fear that new relationships will be ended before they are given a chance to blossom. But keeping such a secret is a burden since we naturally yearn to tell of our struggles and successes to new people in our lives. And if we remain silent, we are unable to educate others in our communities about the fact that people do recover and have productive lives.

In safe environments, I will reveal my burdensome secret to feel free and educate others.

No rose without a thorn.—French proverb

We who live in recovery have experienced both suffering and beauty. We have known pain and confusion, but we also know of the power of recovery. As a result, we have learned to be more compassionate toward others and ourselves. Through our compassion, we can reach out to others who are living with mental illnesses and encourage them to take a step toward recovery—a vibrant, colorful rose.

I am willing to share the rose of recovery with others.

It is by believing in roses that one brings them to bloom.—
French proverb

We can define recovery as the process for improving our lives. It doesn't mean that our mental illnesses disappear. Recovery is a winding, bumpy road and to travel it requires vigilance, dedication, and hope. Our first step to achieving recovery is to believe recovery is possible. We have the potential to participate in life, and that despite our obstacles we can achieve. It is this belief in recovery that can make it a reality.

I will believe in recovery so it will become a reality in my life.

No one is expected to achieve the impossible.—French proverb

Let us set realistic goals for ourselves. Today, it may mean attending one class. Some of us may be able to attend four classes today. Tomorrow we may be completing a ten-page paper or one paragraph. We are all different. We, and no one else, get to decide what is possible and impossible in our lives. Wisdom and experience can guide us to realistic goals for the day, week, month, and year. If our goals are realistic, we may not have to deal with disappointments. If our goals are realistic, and we accomplish them, we will see ourselves as successes.

We grow through our efforts and no one can expect us to achieve the impossible.

To turn an obstacle to one's advantage is a great step towards victory.—French proverb

Although we don't normally view a mental illness as being advantageous to us, we can elect to see that our coping with mental illness is a great step toward victory. We have defeated our symptoms in the past and kept it at a distance for long periods using various coping skills such as writing, painting, seeking professional assistance, or exercising. So, when symptoms enter our lives again, our successes in the past reassure us that our debilitating symptoms can go away again when we implement our coping skills.

My coping skills are a great step toward victory in combating the symptoms of mental illness.

A man's fortune must first be changed within.—Chinese proverb

Although many facets of our lives including work, finances, and relationships have been impacted by mental illness, we can improve our situations through our attitudes and inner strength. Other people may guide us to recovery, but we are the ones who choose whether to venture down its path. Through our determination and inner strength, our lives improve once we discover and follow the path to recovery.

My inner strength and determination will lead me down the road of recovery and my life will then improve.

LORETTE M. ENOCHS

A journey of a thousand miles must begin with a single step.—Chinese proverb

Our lifelong journey of recovery begins with a single step: acceptance. Acceptance involves three streets that intersect: individual acceptance, familial acceptance, and societal acceptance. Our denial of our illness, as well as society's and some family members' prejudices or inability to accept mental illnesses, is an obstacle that impedes our recovery. We cannot control what others think. Once we step forward on that street of acceptance, we begin our journey of a thousand miles that leads to recovery. On our journey we learn to combat the effects of society's prejudices and ignorance on our lives.

I will begin my journey of recovery with the step of acceptance.

It is better to light a candle than curse the darkness.—
Chinese proverb

Recovery illuminates our world with hope for a better future. Recovery doesn't happen overnight and rarely without some setbacks. But we can trust that recovery does happen and life improves. By accepting recovery in our lives, we ignite candles of hope for a better future.

By lighting a candle of hope, I can see the rainbow of recovery.

LORETTE M. ENOCHS

The man who removes a mountain begins by carrying away small stones—Chinese proverb

Mental illness is a foreboding mountain to be conquered and recovery is like carrying small stones away from that mountain of pain, fear, and distortions. Recovery is an incremental healing process with successes and setbacks. We can remove the worst of our debilitating symptoms through building our personal plan for recovery based on our successes and failures.

The foreboding mountain of mental illness will be reduced to the size of a surmountable hill by carrying away small stones through recovery strategies.

Grow where you are planted.—Latin proverb

We can't change the genetic coding or environmental catalysts that caused our mental illness, but we can grow in the rich soil of recovery in which we can plant ourselves. We can think of recovery as a garden, which needs to be routinely tended so that we can flourish. We shape our own destinies by creating recovery strategies that aid us in our growth. Our tools for recovery might include a journal, teddy bear, phone numbers of our treatment team or friends, an advance directive, or coloring book and crayons. By tending to our garden of recovery, we shall see the flowers and fruits of our efforts.

I will create a recovery toolbox so my life can blossom fully.

Grief pent up will burst the heart.—Italian proverb

If we continually carry our sorrow and do not mourn our losses, we run the risk of being stuck in the past and hindering our recovery. Unresolved grief shrouds the heart in hopelessness. There is no reason to stay in that dark place. By making a list of the things that failed to happen or did happen because mental illness disrupted our lives, we may be able to express our pent-up grief. Allow that grief to surface. Now tear up that list and make another. This time write down what we are going to do to improve our lives today and tomorrow. By virtue of expressing and releasing old pent-up grief then embracing hope for new opportunities, we improve our lives in the present.

I will release the thoughts of what my life could have been and embrace new thoughts of a rewarding life in the future.

A man cannot be comfortable without his own approval.—
Mark Twain

When we approve of ourselves, we are blessing our inner spiritual self. Although we have likely made poor judgments resulting in negative legal, financial, employment, or relationship consequences due to our mental illnesses, we can decide to stop condemning our past behavior and instead pay homage to our inner goodness and beauty, which is the greatest gift we can give ourselves.

I am grateful for my inner goodness and beauty.

Comparisons are odious.—John Lydgate

Comparing our traits and accomplishments to others is harmful and only leads to damage either to us or to other individuals. Such hurtful comparisons are from the voices of others or from our own inner judgmental self—talk that often undermines our self-worth. It is time to shut down the comparison channel in our heads and turn on the affirmation channel which broadcasts messages such as I did the best I could, I'm happy with what I did today, or I'm proud of myself for trying.

I will shut down my comparison channel and turn on the affirmations channel.

There is no more certain sign of a narrow mind, of stupidity and of arrogance than to stand aloof from those who think differently from us.—Walter Savage Landor

Many of us had been ridiculed because we think, feel, see, taste, or hear differently. And many of us have been stared at or avoided because our symptoms erupted in public. If we had a heart attack or were bleeding profusely from an accident in public, compassion would drive strangers to assist. But when symptoms of mental illness surface, few strangers approach with words such as: "Is there anything that I can do to help you?" In my vision of a perfect world, everyone would understand mental illnesses and the study of psychology would be a requirement for a high school diploma. Then maybe all people would know to ask if they could help an individual with a mental illness in his/her darkest moments. It was once said that man would never walk on the moon. But what may have seemed impossible became a reality. Consequently, I can dare to dream that in the future all people will have understanding and compassion for people living with mental illness.

I hope that someday there will be universal understanding and compassion for those living with mental illnesses.

I was successful because you believed in me.—Ulysses
S. Grant

Ulysses S. Grant succeeded because he had half a country and its belief system—all men are created equal—on his side. The belief others have in us can be a catalyst for our success in recovery. Let us take time today to appreciate those who have supported us on our journey of recovery—friends, family, therapists, group leaders, or perhaps even a stranger who spoke words of encouragement as we fought the symptoms of our disorders. Without their encouragement, we may not have been able to advance our recovery.

I thank individuals who told me that they believed in my recovery and me.

I was successful because I believed in me.—LME

Self-confidence propels us into action, permits us to seek new relationships, and guides us to new adventures and accomplishments. Yet sometimes self-confidence plays hide and seek within our inner self and we have to coax it to surface. Fear can undermine our self-confidence so it is necessary to fight fears. We can bolster our self-confidence by telling ourselves that we are worthy and deserve new relationships and productive adventures. Believing in self is the first step to achieving our goals.

I believe in my successfulness and self.

*The friend in my adversity I shall always cherish the most.
I can better trust those who helped to relieve the gloom of
my dark hours than those who are so ready to enjoy with
me the sunshine of my prosperity*—Ulysses S. Grant

When the raging invisible pain paralyzed us or confusion interfered with our ability to function, we are indebted to the people who understood mental illness and promised us that life would improve. How can we ever repay that person who stood by us during our darkest moment—perhaps a friend, relative, or therapist? I am indebted to the person who asked me to give life a chance and told me that recovery was possible. The candles of hope they gave me sustained me through the darkest hours.

I thank those people who helped and guided me on my journey of recovery.

Every human being, of whatever origin, of whatever station, deserves respect. We must each respect others even as we respect ourselves.—Ulysses S. Grant

Many of us have been dismissed because we have a mental illness. "She's the crazy one of the family," a relative says. "He's a patient," explains a nurse as she rolls her eyes. But people living with mental illnesses deserve the same respect as other humans. We deserve respect for our ability to survive the chaotic and intense moments of our lives. We deserve respect for accepting our differences and moving forward in our recovery. We deserve respect for surviving societal stigma associated with the label mental illness. We can respect ourselves for the same reasons others should be respecting us. Such self-respect may someday blossom into a mental illness pride movement. Just as the gay community has rainbow pride, maybe one day we'll have a silver ribbon pride movement to eliminate the prejudices against people living with mental illnesses. Time and movement are on our side.

I respect myself for my ability to move forward and anticipate the day when individuals with mental illness are given the respect they deserve by others.

I am not now That which I have been.—Lord Byron

Time, the world, and recovery are in constant motion. The introduction of recovery into our lives changes us, teaching us that we can heal. Through recovery, we learn about our potential and capabilities as well as about the important roles of hope, effort, and support. Through recovery, we create tools to buoy us in future rough seas. We learn that we can and do heal. Through healing, we can have fruitful relationships with our family, friends, co-workers, or partners or engage in activities that we enjoy such as producing music or art, playing sports, or writing.

Recovery transforms my life.

I cannot think that we are useless or God would not have created us. There is one God looking down on us all. We are all the children of one God. The sun, the darkness, the winds are all listening to what we have to say. –Geronimo

No man or woman is useless. We all have purpose in life. We are children, friends, neighbors, workers, parents, or students. God has breathed His/Her spirit of life unto us. He/She has empowered us with the capacity to endure our suffering and to celebrate a life of recovery. Through the gift of recovery, we have been given a new voice that allows us to engage in healthier relationships and to inform others that recovery is possible.

My Higher Power has given me purpose to my life—recovery.

While living I want to live well.—Geronimo

Living well means living to the best of our abilities. For those living with a mental illness, acceptance is a key factor in living a good life. Acceptance opens us up to the possibility of recovery. Acceptance allows us to receive education and wisdom into our lives, which can guide us in our recovery. Acceptance offers us a biological or environmental reason for our extraordinary behavior. Let us embrace acceptance and recovery and welcome sanity into our lives.

I will practice acceptance to live well.

Without a struggle, there can be no progress.—Frederick Douglass

We struggle when our symptoms unexpectedly erupt and potentially usher chaos into our lives. We fight for breath to survive the undercurrents of the black sea of our symptoms that drag us away from the steady shores of recovery. Fortunately, we've learned mental health recovery skills to stem off total catastrophe. Each relapse has taught us new ways of managing our disorders. We recover again and again with greater ease because of the tools that we have learned. It is our struggles that highlight our progress.

I will weather the struggles of my mental illness because I have set sail on the journey of recovery.

The best safety lies in fear.—William Shakespeare

Fear propels us instinctively to seek safety. A safe environment allows us to deal better with our mental illnesses. Although we hope that it will not be necessary to seek a safe environment for our recovery, it is best to be prepared by identifying an environment where we can heal. We may seek safety at a drop-in center, friend's house, a therapist's office, or hospital room. An advance directive is a safety tool that tells other what we need and want to assist in our recovery.

I will make plans for my future by drafting a safety plan so that I can have my wishes for recovery heard.

I could not tread these perilous paths in safety, if I did not keep a saving sense of humor.— Horatio Nelson

Humor is a release valve for our pent-up emotions. When we are living them, our dark experiences are not humorous. However, in retrospect and in the company of the right friends, we may be able to look back and find humor in some aspects of our mental illnesses. My friends and I who live with mental illnesses find humor in some parts of our adventures caused by mania and delusions. After all, there is humor in the activities of two adult women scouting out a neighborhood late at night with the intention of cutting flowers from neighbors' flowerbeds—one cutting, the other driving the get-away car. Or, the night individuals snatched the school superintendent's garbage and sifted through his discarded papers, sleuthing for information. (It was one of those brilliant, manic ideas. Surely, Nancy Drew and Sherlock Holmes, my childhood heroes would have applauded me.) If we can laugh at our extreme behavior occasionally, it can assist recovery.

I will laugh today to assist my recovery.

No great thing is created suddenly.—Epictetus

Flowers start with a seed. The seed develops roots, stalk, and leaves with the aid of water, soil, and sunshine. Time and nutrients are the catalysts for flowers to blossom. Our recovery is a gradual process like that of a plant's growth. It begins with someone planting a seed that recovery is possible. We develop roots in our community by interacting with groups, therapists, healers, or psychiatrists. The stem of recovery grows from these rooting. Eventually, recovery is not just one blossom in our life but an entire garden.

My life is a garden of recovery.

Kindness is a language which the deaf can hear and the blind can see.—Mark Twain

Kindness is a universal language that can penetrate the most confused mind. Kindness creates a bond. Kindness is a quality that we seek in our friends and family and we can bestow upon others and ourselves. A word of encouragement, of acceptance, and of understanding lifts our spirits and provides the wind beneath our wings, allowing us to soar to new heights of recovery.

Today I will be kind to myself as well as to others.

If you add a little to a little, and then do it again, soon that little shall be much. –Hesiod

Recovery occurs gradually. We begin with belief; add acceptance and then action. By these steps, we are on the path to recovery. Now, take another step. We can try to stretch beyond what we believe is our ability today, and successfully leap over another hurdle. Or, we may elect to stay on a path of small steps of recovery. Although recovery is incremental and may take more time than we want, it is unstoppable as long as we believe, accept our lives as they can be and take action.

I know that recovery is usually gradual and requires my belief, acceptance, and action, and I will take these steps.

Life can only be understood backwards, but it must be lived forward.—Soren Kierkegaard

For those of us who are living with a mental illness, our pasts are filled with extreme behaviors that we wish we could forget. Through education about our mental illnesses, we have learned that the causes of our extreme behaviors were attributable to biochemical imbalances of the brain or traumatic event. By forgiving our past behavior and embracing the principles of recovery, we are able to move forward.

I will not dwell in the past other than to reflect upon the lessons that I've learned. My life of recovery belongs to today and tomorrow.

LORETTE M. ENOCHS

Thought is the sculptor who can create the person you want to be.—Henry David Thoreau

Our thoughts are sculptors. We can change our life circumstances by altering our thoughts. Through positive thoughts, we cast a light of hope that will brighten our future. When the darkness of defeatism powers the windmills of our mind, causing our thoughts to become negative, we can use the power of our positive thoughts to envelop our mind with hope and change our circumstances for the better. We can also use positive thoughts to design our self-image. If we believe that we are inferior, then we act inferior. If we accept that we have value, then we act accordingly. If we believe that we are beautiful, we will create a beautiful image by caring for our appearance. And the more we care for our appearance, the more our minds respond with a positive self-image and people respond more positively to us. In turn, such positive responses from others create an even stronger self-image.

No matter how badly I feel I will try to think positive thoughts and dress to impress in order to generate a positive self-image and positive responses from others.

To dare is to lose one's footing momentarily. To not dare is to lose oneself.—Soren Kierkegaard

Recovery is risky. To achieve it, we must dare to lose our footing momentarily and take a leap of faith that our lives will improve if we adopt recovery principles of acceptance, nurture, and vigilance. Recovery requires us to let go of the known and move into the unfamiliar territory. There is no steady footing on the road to recovery. Each person who chooses this path must find his/her own way by trial and error. There is pain involved as we examine our pasts so we can make positive changes in the future. But rarely is there growth without pain. Let's dare to look beyond the fear of pain and embrace the changes that will positively alter our lives.

I will dare to lose my footing momentarily to find recovery.

*What a man thinks of himself, that it is which determines,
or rather indicates his fate.*—Henry David Thoreau

We who live with mental illness have experienced shame because we have acted or thought differently or because people who don't understand our circumstances have whispered judgmental words. But we have the power to overcome our thoughts of shame and protect ourselves from judgmental words. We are not our disorder. We are individuals who cope well with hereditary or traumatic conditions. We will not allow mental illness to consume our lives, but instead we will manage it. We can blast the words of shame to the distant corners of our minds by pursuing art, work, music, athletics, advocacy, or anything else that brings us happiness and a sense of fulfillment.

I will think of myself positively in order to have a hopeful future.

Tears are the safety valve of the heart when too much pressure is laid on it.—Albert Smith

Tears are cleansing. Let us welcome both tears of sadness and joy in our lives. Some of us have been shamed because we dared to express our emotions rather than deny our feelings. When tears appear in our eyes, let us affirm our feelings. We have reasons for our sadness: we have experienced many losses. We have reasons for our joy: we have had to jump over mind-boggling hurdles to achieve. Our physical and mental health will prosper because of the tears that have rolled down our faces, releasing the pressures of the heart.

Like sunshine and storms, I will welcome tears in my life to release life's pressures.

As soon as you trust yourself, you will know how to live.—
Johann Wolfgang von Goethe

Our mental illnesses have shaken us to our cores. An internal volcanic eruption has spilled, hot, steamy lava onto our life's journey. The emergence of toxic, acid-filled clouds of delusion and reactive emotion altered our ability to decipher reality. Our ability to think and express emotions has been impaired. Our minds have cascaded into confusion and self-doubt. But recovery dissipates the clouds of confusion and self-doubt. On the journey of recovery, we begin to trust ourselves again—memories are sharper, information is processed more accurately, and our emotions cease to fluctuate between high peaks and low canyons.

As I travel on the road to recovery, I will trust myself to make good decisions that will keep me from harm's way.

The two most powerful warriors are patience and time.—
Leo Tolstoy

In order for us to live well, we combat the symptoms of our mental illnesses. Our two most powerful warriors in our battle are patience and time. Since medications or wellness strategies usually do not provide instant relief, patience and time become vital to our recovery. We who are in recovery know from experience that the trial and error process of recovery is often frustrating, tiring, and time-consuming. But we also acknowledge that both patience and time eventually lead us to recovery.

Patience and time give me the best chances for recovery.

Nothing endures but change. Heraclitus

Change is constant; it is unavoidable. Nonetheless, we often resist change. Our anxiety amplifies when change occurs. However, our attitude about change can reduce our anxiety. We can welcome positive changes in our lives, and attempt to remedy change that negatively impacts our lives. Sometimes we cannot control what occurs in our lives, and surrendering to events beyond our control may be our only survival option. Our inner wisdom suggests to us when it time for welcoming or surrendering.

By wisely welcoming change or surrendering to it, I will do more than endure. I will thrive.

Lorette M. Enochs

People are crying up the rich and variegated plumage of the peacock, and he himself is blushing at his feet.— Shaiku Sa'di Shirazi

Seldom do we see our own beauty or applaud ourselves for being creative, sensitive, and resilient individuals who are on the path of recovery. Unfortunately, we often focus on our blemishes—our symptoms of mental illness. When we allow our shame associated with our diagnosis to take hold of our psyche, it impedes our ability to appreciate our inner beauty. Once we have released our shame and negative thoughts concerning our diagnosis, we are free to enjoy our rich and variegated plumage of inner beauty.

I am in awe of my own inner beauty and I will acknowledge it whenever shame enters my psyche.

LORETTE M. ENOCHS

If a man does not keep pace with his companions, perhaps it is because he hears a different drummer. Let him step to the music which he hears, however measured or far away.—Henry David Thoreau

We who are in recovery hear different drummers and step to our own music, each finding our own way to wellness. But because another person living with mental illness is not on our road to recovery doesn't mean he has gotten lost—he is simply traveling his own road at his own speed, with his individual capabilities. Being an example of wellness is the best encouragement that we can give others who seek recovery.

I will step to the music of recovery, which I hear.

I am more and more convinced that our happiness or our unhappiness depends far more on the way we meet the events of life than on the nature of those events themselves.— Karl Wilhelm von Humboldt

Mental illness has altered our lives, impacting our abilities to process information, gauge our emotions well, work effectively, build relationships, or manage our finances. But ultimately our happiness and achievement will depend on the attitudes we have about rebuilding our lives. By creating and implementing plans for our recovery, happiness will emerge in our lives. We can rebuild our relationships, manage our finances better, and achieve.

I will maintain positive attitudes toward living with a mental illness and the possibilities for recovery.

Tears are the silent language of grief. Voltaire

Grief and anger are normal responses to being diagnosed with a mental illness. We have every right to experience such emotions. Our lives have been altered so that we are now primarily focused on wellness while all other goals become secondary. Unless we strive for wellness, we limit our ability to do other rewarding activities such as art or sports. To strive for wellness, we need to take time to shed two types of tears: tears of grief because we have been diagnosed with a mental illness and tears of joy because we know recovery is possible.

My tears are cleansing and promote wellness.

LORETTE M. ENOCHS

The ancestor of every action is a thought.—Ralph Waldo Emerson

Our thoughts affect our actions. When we think positively, we act positively. When we think negatively, we act negatively. Transforming our thoughts so that we avoid being sucked into the vortex of negativity requires a conscious decision to think of better ways to handle the difficulties that arise in our lives so that we can achieve better outcomes. We can be our own spin-doctors by adopting recovery principles of positive thoughts. When we allow recovery principles to guide our actions, our lives improve.

I will be my own spin-doctor and create a recovery plan to guide me through difficult times.

An ironic truth is that positive change often results from chaos. LME

Mental illness often creates chaos in our lives. Our chaotic thoughts sometimes resulted in major losses. We sometimes lose friends and jobs. We may spend money unwisely. We may tax our relationships with family members. Yet, recovery introduces positive change in our lives. Recovery offers us the opportunity for improving our lives and creating new relationships or repairing old ones. Recovery allows us to learn new coping skills to reduce the likelihood of chaos bursting into our lives again.

Recovery is a welcome, positive change in my life.

Small minds are concerned with the extraordinary, great minds with the ordinary.—Blaise Pascal

People who stigmatize individuals living with mental illnesses are small minds, while those who accept that the ordinary ability of the mind to think differently have great minds. We who live with mental illnesses rarely think of ourselves as ordinary, yet mental illness is so prevalent that it can be seen as an ordinary. We are among the company of many who experience extreme yet common thoughts and emotions.

I will surround myself with great minds of acceptance.

Man: Half dust half deity.— Lord Byron

A Higher Power created us in His/Her image. So the Divine is within us. The Spirit of Love is the Divine. Some of us think that no one will love us due to our mental illness diagnosis. We must discard those negative thoughts that hinder us from our inherent potential to love and be loved, and embrace the knowledge that we are worthy of loving and being loved. When we open ourselves up to the possibility of loving relationships, we will create loving bonds.

Because I was created in the image of my Higher Power, and the Divine is within me, I am worthy of love and to be loved.

Many things are lost for want of asking.—English proverb

We do not have to be alone in our journey of recovery. We can reach out to others for help: psychiatrists, psychologists, social workers, therapists, friends, family, or groups. We can learn much from others, particularly from those who live with mental illnesses and walk on the path of recovery. Once we accept that asking for help is a sign of strength not weakness, we are more likely to seek guidance and support during our most difficult times.

I will ask for help when I feel overwhelmed or isolated.

He who conceals his disease cannot expect to be cured. –Ethiopian proverb

We often hide our diagnosis for fear that others will think less of us or out of shame. But finding the path to recovery requires a willingness to divulge our symptoms to those who can help us. Our unwillingness to share our conditions with those who can help us hampers our recovery. It may be easier to seek help if we acknowledge that mental illnesses are common and many talented individuals have lived successful lives because they sought help.

I will reach out to those who can be members of my recovery team.

Far away there in the sunshine are my highest aspirations. I may not reach them, but I can look up and see their beauty, believe in them, and try to follow where they lead.—Louisa May Alcott

Our aspirations sustain us and fan the flames of hope. Without hope, our world is as desolate as a moon crater. We aspire for a meaningful life filled with loving relationships, a rewarding job in the fields of art, music, writing, business, athletics, or other activities that interest us. Because of our aspirations, we strive to be well so that we can achieve our heart's desires. Although some of us may never reach the goals to which we aspire, our lives have meaning because we choose to follow our aspirations.

My aspirations inspire me to be well so that I can achieve my goals.

Suicide is not a remedy. –James Garfield

Many of us living with a mental illness have erroneously thought that death was a better option than life. Our invisible pain can be unbearable. This can lead our thoughts to take dangerous detours, whereby death is considered as an alternative to our pain. Sometimes it seems as though we cannot escape these dangerous thoughts, but it is possible to change them. By seeking aid, we can find safety so that we can know the joys of tomorrow.

I will seek safety and aid so that I can know the joys of tomorrow.

And the day came when the risk to remain tight in a bud was more painful than the risk it took to blossom.—
Anais Nin

The pain of living with our symptoms can be unbearable, yet fear of the unknown holds us in our present pain. Once we have released the fear of trying new strategies for recovery, recovery blossoms. Recovery requires trust. Trust requires belief and a willingness to set off on a path of change, not knowing with certainty what we will encounter on that path. We should welcome the time in our recovery when the risk to remain as we are is more painful than the risk to blossom because this will move us forward.

I will let recovery blossom in my life.

LORETTE M. ENOCHS

It's not what you call me, but what I answer to. –African proverb

When people call us mentally ill we do not need to answer this label. Mental illness is only a small part of our existence. We are like everyone else except that we live with a brain disorder and strive for a better life through recovery. We are the sum of our dreams, aspirations, abilities, talents, and struggles. We will call ourselves people in recovery and we shall answer to that.

I will not allow myself to be limited by labels given me by those who are ignorant or prejudiced.

Re-examine all you have been told . . . dismiss what insults your soul.—Walt Whitman

Some of us have been told that our lives are over because of our diagnosis. How dare such people condemn us to such a fate! Our lives have meaning despite being interrupted and altered by mental illness. Our wants and desires to achieve are no different than those living with no mental illness. The possibility of recovery is real and offers us opportunities to achieve. We may move slower to achieve, but we can succeed.

I will not allow the naysayers to insult my soul.

LORETTE M. ENOCHS

I'm not afraid of storms, for I'm learning how to sail my ship.—Louisa May Alcott

As we learn to monitor and manage our symptoms, we have less to fear. Recovery plans can reduce the length of time we have difficulties. Relaxation exercises might improve our sleep; a schedule may reduce the possibility of our symptoms erupting; cognitive behavioral therapy practices provide us with tools for positive thinking. By creating a written recovery plan we have a script to follow when the storm clouds of mental illness begin to reappear on the horizon.

I will create a recovery plan for when the storm clouds of mental illness reappear on the horizon.

One ship drives east another drives west
With the self-same winds that blow.
'Tis the set of the sails,
And not the gales
That tell them the way to go. – Ella Wheeler Wilcox

We are the navigators of our own destiny. With recovery as our sails, we can escape the ravaging currents, hurricane winds, and tsunami waves of mental illness. By implementing a recovery plan, we can steer away from the symptoms that debilitate us. We search for clear skies and smooth sailing. We are the captains of our futures.

Recovery and I are shipmates, setting the sails for success.

Lorette M. Enochs

We never know how high we are
Till we are called to rise;
And then, if we are true to plan,
Our statures touch the skies. – Emily Dickinson

Our difficulties with mental illness call upon us to summon our inner strength and resiliency. Sometimes the task of recovery seems impossible, but our belief in recovery pushes us to find a way to wellness. We should all be given medals of bravery for our courage to accept our condition and move forward on our path of recovery, even though our obstacles seem insurmountable at times. Our capacity to persist is a measure of our strength and an indication of our stature.

I will summon inner strength to keep my stature high.

As long as I can breathe, change for the better is a possibility.—LME

Life constantly evolves. Just as the seasons change from the icy cold of winter to the sunny warmth of summer, our lives change. When we are feeling our worst, we can embrace the belief that life will improve. Our belief in positive change is a life preserver that can keep us afloat during our darkest hours. Ask ourselves what can we change today that will be a catalyst for improving our lives tomorrow. We can make an appointment with our therapists; create a collage of how we are feeling; write our stories; telephone a family member or friend who can support us through our difficult time; take out our recovery plan; search for housing; or engage in another positive activity that can bring about change.

I will hold on to the belief that change is possible during my darkest moments and take one small step toward improving my life today.

Reject your sense of injury and the injury itself disappears.
Marcus Aurelius Antonius

Many of us have been emotionally hurt due to intentional or neglectful acts or inactions of others. An apology may never be forthcoming. We cannot change others' behavior. We can only change our attitudes about the wrong that was done to us. By holding unto the pain of those injuries, we limit our ability to heal. Forgiveness is healing. Forgiveness allows us to break the bond of resentment that ties us to the person who injured us. By forgiving, we move beyond our resentment.

By forgiving, my injury can disappear.

"No man is an island. . ." John Donne

We who live with mental illnesses fight the demon called isolation. Our illnesses or shame may drive us to isolate. It may be too overwhelming to interact with others. Even when we elect to isolate, we often yearn to have companionship. A healthy relationship breathes fulfillment into our souls. It nurtures us, giving us opportunities to expand emotionally and intellectually. How do we overcome the demon of isolation that hinders our ability to create healthy relationships? We can take that first step out the door. We can attend groups for those living with mental illnesses. Each time that we connect with another person, we open the door for companionship.

I am ready to leave my island of isolation to build healthy relationships.

When we speak we are afraid our words will not be heard or welcomed. But when we are silent, we are still afraid. So it is better to speak.—Audre Lorde

Sometimes we remain silent about our needs or the system's failures because of our fear that individuals will think less of us or deny us services that we request. Those fears sometimes paralyze us into silent submission, sabotaging our recovery. By taking a risk and voicing our needs, recovery can blossom in our lives.

For sanity's sake I will exercise speaking my mind with gentle words.

Your life is a story. The miracle of your life unfolds one moment at a time.— LME

There is no question that those who live with mental illnesses have had many moments in their lives filled with hardship, but those yesterdays are gone. Let us acknowledge that troublesome moments may surface again in the future, but we will be better prepared to cope with them. To dwell on hardships in the present ruins our chance to have a better today. In this moment, take a deep breath and recognize that you are a miracle. Try to hold that thought whenever thoughts of hardship surface.

My life is a miracle.

Lorette M. Enochs

Printed in the United States
By Bookmasters